Cute monsters heads

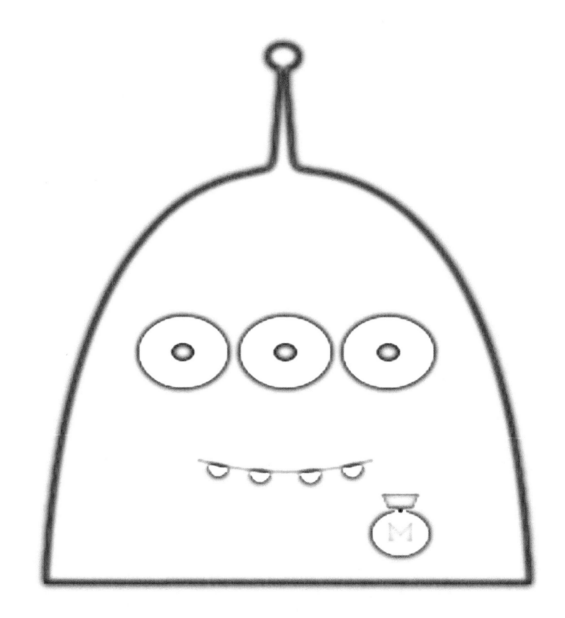

GIVE ME A COLORFUL NAME

....

GIVE ME A COLORFUL NAME

. . . .

GIVE ME A COLORFUL NAME

....

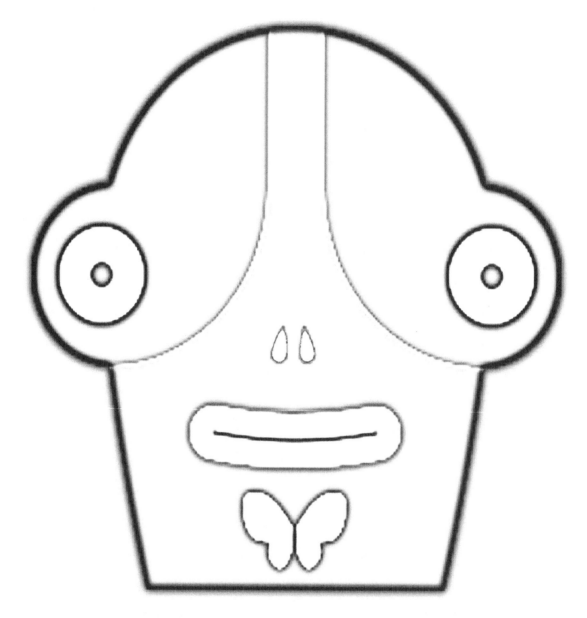

GIVE ME A COLORFUL NAME

....

GIVE ME A COLORFUL NAME

. . . .

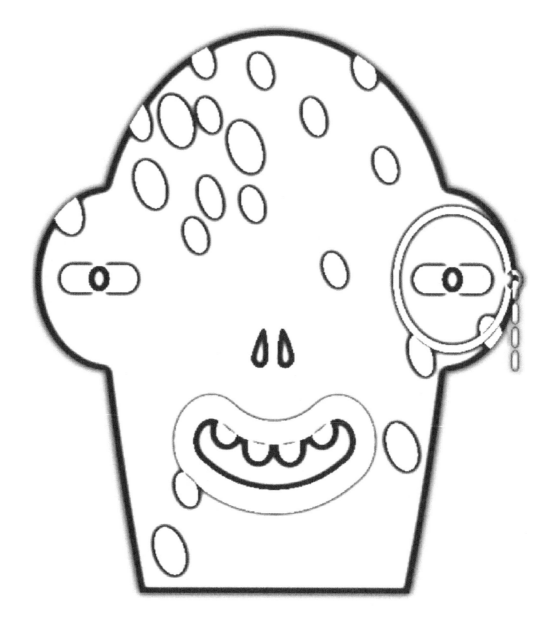

GIVE ME A COLORFUL NAME

- -

GIVE ME A COLORFUL NAME

....

GIVE ME A COLORFUL NAME

....

GIVE ME A COLORFUL NAME

....

GIVE ME A COLORFUL NAME

....

GIVE ME A COLORFUL NAME

....

GIVE ME A COLORFUL NAME

....

GIVE ME A COLORFUL NAME

. . . .

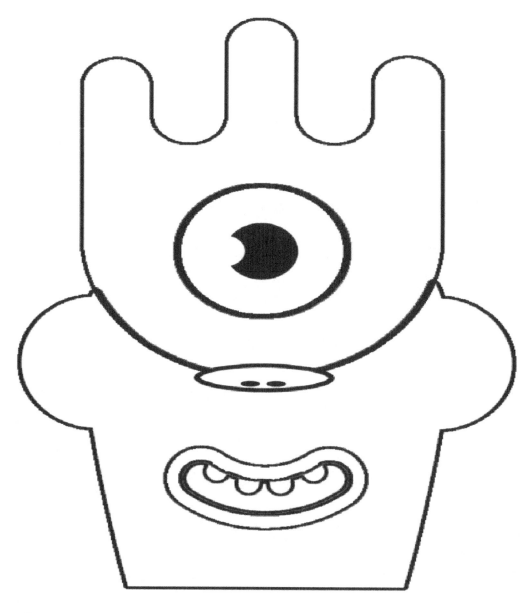

GIVE ME A COLORFUL NAME

- -

GIVE ME A COLORFUL NAME

....

GIVE ME A COLORFUL NAME

....

GIVE ME A COLORFUL NAME

GIVE ME A COLORFUL NAME

- -

GIVE ME A COLORFUL NAME

GIVE ME A COLORFUL NAME

....

GIVE ME A COLORFUL NAME

. . . .

GIVE ME A COLORFUL NAME

- -

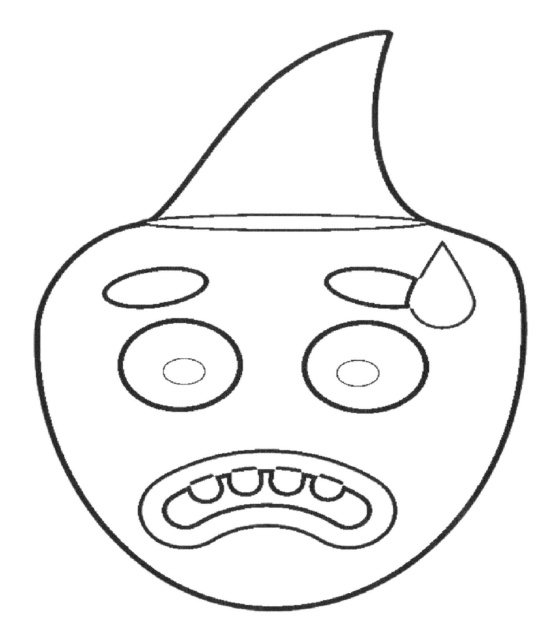

GIVE ME A COLORFUL NAME

GIVE ME A COLORFUL NAME

. . . .

GIVE ME A COLORFUL NAME

....

GIVE ME A COLORFUL NAME

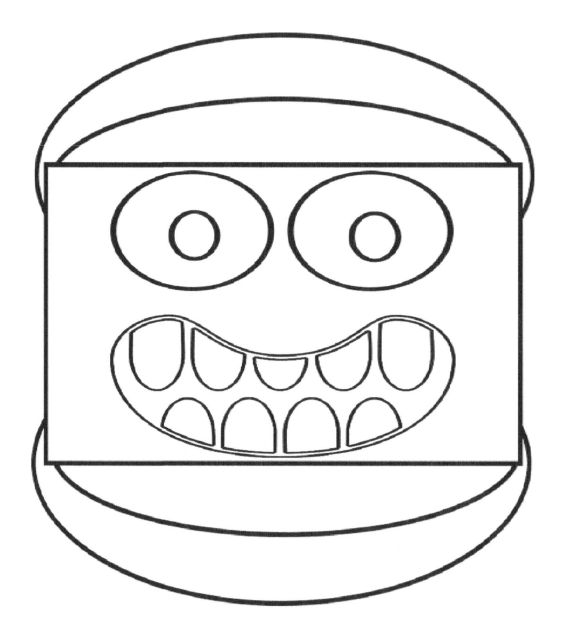

GIVE ME A COLORFUL NAME

....

GIVE ME A COLORFUL NAME

....

GIVE ME A COLORFUL NAME

....

GIVE ME A COLORFUL NAME

....

GIVE ME A COLORFUL NAME

. . . .

GIVE ME A COLORFUL NAME

....

GIVE ME A COLORFUL NAME

. . . .

GIVE ME A COLORFUL NAME

....

GIVE ME A COLORFUL NAME

....

GIVE ME A COLORFUL NAME

. . . .

GIVE ME A COLORFUL NAME

....

GIVE ME A COLORFUL NAME

....

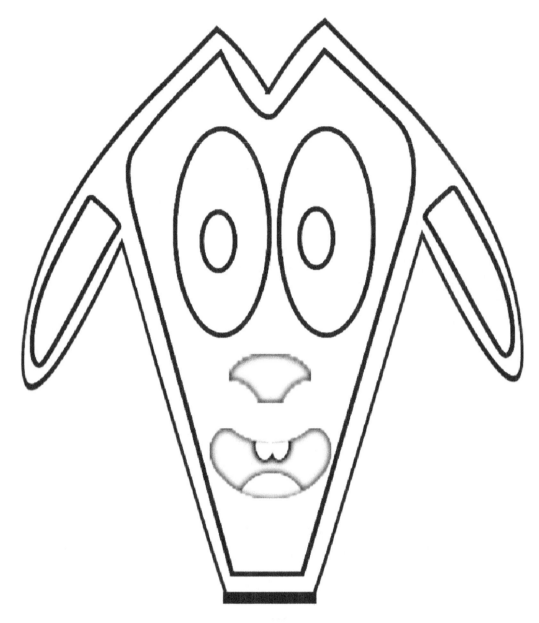

GIVE ME A COLORFUL NAME

....

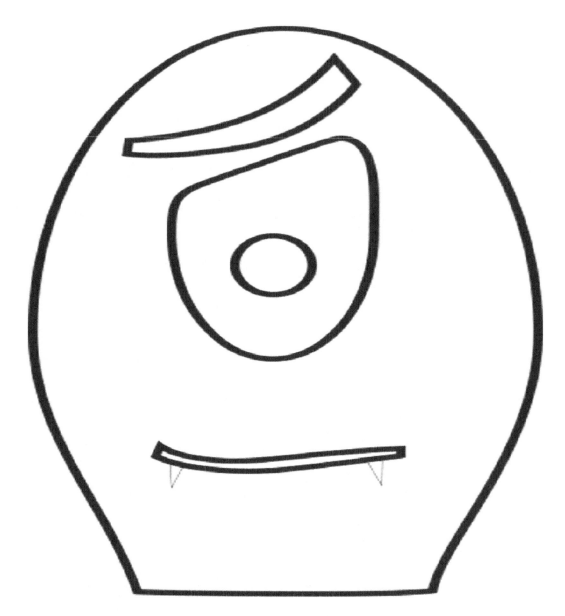

GIVE ME A COLORFUL NAME

....

GIVE ME A COLORFUL NAME

. . . .

GIVE ME A COLORFUL NAME

....

GIVE ME A COLORFUL NAME

. . . .

GIVE ME A COLORFUL NAME

. . . .

GIVE ME A COLORFUL NAME

....

GIVE ME A COLORFUL NAME

....

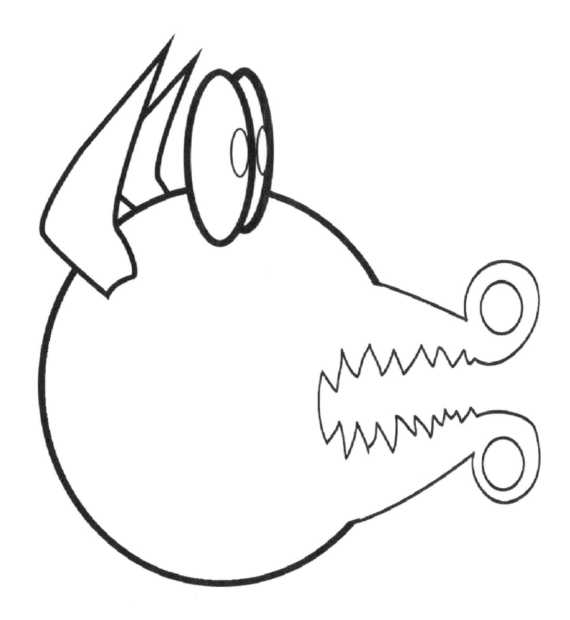

GIVE ME A COLORFUL NAME

·· ·· ·· ·· ·· ·· ·· ·· ·· ·· ·· ·· ·· ·· ··

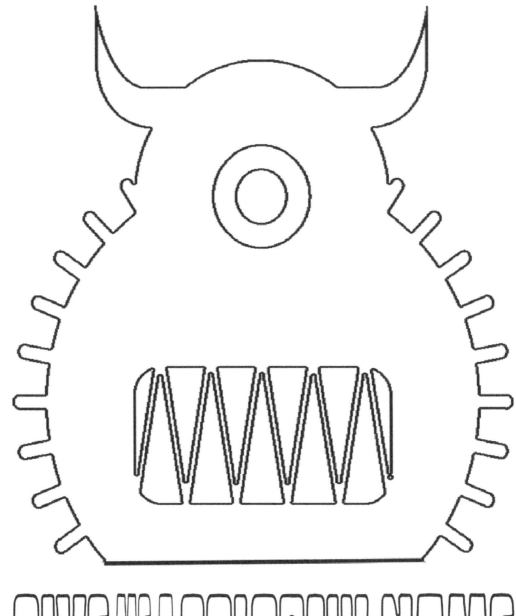

GIVE ME A COLORFUL NAME

....

GIVE ME A COLORFUL NAME

GIVE ME A COLORFUL NAME

. . . .

Made in the USA
Monee, IL
25 October 2022

16525897R00057